JANICE VANCLEAVE'S
FIRST-PLACE SCIENCE FAIR PROJECTS™

STEP-BY-STEP
SCIENCE EXPERIMENTS IN
EARTH SCIENCE

rosen publishing's
rosen
central®

NEW YORK

This edition first published in 2013 by:

The Rosen Publishing Group, Inc.
29 East 21st Street
New York, NY 10010

Library of Congress Cataloging-in-Publication Data

VanCleave, Janice Pratt.
Step-by-step science experiments in earth science/Janice VanCleave.
    p. cm. — (Janice Vancleave's first-place science fair projects)
Includes bibliographical references and index.
ISBN 978-1-4488-6983-1 (lib. bdg.) — ISBN 978-1-4488-8467-4 (pbk.) —
ISBN 978-1-4488-8468-1 (6-pack)
1. Earth sciences — Experiments — Juvenile literature. I. Title.
QE29.V364 2013
550.78 — dc23

                                                                2012007944

Manufactured in the United States of America

CPSIA Compliance Information: Batch #S12YA: For further information, contact Rosen Publishing, New York, New York, at 1-800-237-9932.

This edition published by arrangement with and permission of John Wiley & Sons, Inc., Hoboken, New Jersey.

Originally published as *Earth Science for Every Kid*. Copyright © 1991 by John Wiley & Sons, Inc.

CONTENTS

INTRODUCTION

Scientists theorize that Earth is about 4.6 billion years old. They know this through studying rocks and minerals, some of the oldest substances on Earth. But since its initial formation, Earth has been constantly changing. Mountain ranges have sprung from the surface; oceans have formed. As Earth evolved, it became able to sustain life. Life on Earth began about three billion years ago with the appearance of one-celled organisms. Scientists have discovered this through the study of fossils. Earth science is essentially the study of Earth. It combines physics, chemistry, biology, astronomy, and geology. Studying earth science, like studying all sciences, is a way of solving problems and discovering why things happen the way they do. How was Earth formed? How is it changing? How is life sustained on Earth? These are all questions that have been answered through the study of earth science and its individual branches.

It seems that humans have always tried to explain the world around them. In early Greek myth, the movement of the sun across the sky was attributed to Apollo (the sun god) pulling it with his chariot. Thunderbolts were thrown by Zeus, the king of the gods, to express his anger. Volcanoes were attributed to Hephaestus, the god of fire. As time went by, the myths changed and were spread through the tradition of storytelling. The Romans had their own versions of the Greek gods, later replaced by one god with the rise of Christianity. These myths explained events that were observed but not understood. As time passed, each generation gathered new information and facts, and slowly, knowledge about Earth has been accumulated. Scientific fact has slowly overtaken mythological explanation, although many cultures around the world still attribute natural phenomena to godlike forces.

The wonderful fact that there is still so very much to learn and understand should excite all young scientists and encourage them to seek answers to unsolved problems and question things presented as fact. Scientists identify a problem and seek solutions through research and experimentation. Science began and continues due to our own curiosity. This book may not lead to any new scientific discoveries, but it will provide fun experiments that teach known earth science concepts.

This book will help you make the most of the exciting scientific era in which we live. It will guide you in discovering answers to many questions relating to earth science. The answers will be discovered by performing the fun, safe, and workable experiments in this book.

You will be rewarded with successful experiments if you read an experiment carefully, follow each step in order, and do not substitute equipment. It is suggested that the experiments within a group be performed in order. There is some buildup of information from the first to the last, but any terms defined in a previous experiment can be found in the glossary. A goal of this book is to guide you through the steps necessary in successfully completing a science experiment and to teach you the best method of solving problems and discovering answers. The following list gives the standard pattern for each experiment in the book:

1. **PURPOSE:** This states the basic goals for the experiment.
2. **MATERIALS:** A list of necessary supplies.
3. **PROCEDURE:** Step-by-step instructions on how to perform the experiment.
4. **RESULTS:** An explanation stating exactly what is expected to happen. This is an immediate learning tool. If the expected results are achieved, the experimenter has an immediate positive reinforcement. An error is also quickly recognized, and the need to start over or make corrections is readily apparent.
5. **WHY?:** An explanation of why the results were achieved is described in understandable terms. This means understandable to the reader who may not be familiar with scientific terms.

General Instructions for the Reader
1. Read first. Read each experiment completely before starting.
2. Collect needed supplies. You will experience less frustration and more fun if all the necessary materials for the

experiments are ready for instant use. You lose your train of thought when you have to stop and search for supplies.

3. Experiment. Follow each step very carefully, never skip steps, and do not add your own. Safety is of the utmost importance, and by reading any experiment before starting, then following the instructions exactly, you can feel confident that no unexpected results will occur.

4. Observe. If your results are not the same as described in the experiment, carefully reread the instructions, and start over from the first step.

Most important, remember to have fun!

BULGING BALL

PURPOSE: To determine why the earth bulges at the equator.

MATERIALS:

- construction paper— 16 inches (40 cm) long
- scissors
- paper hole punch
- ruler
- paper glue
- pencil

PROCEDURE:

1. Cut two separate strips, 1¼ in. × 16 in. (3 cm × 40 cm), from construction paper.
2. Cross the strips at their centers and glue.

3. Bring the four
ends together,
overlap, and glue,
forming a sphere.

4. Allow the glue to dry.

5. Cut a hole through the center of the overlapped ends with
the hole punch.

6. Push about 2 in. (5 cm) of the pencil through the hole.
7. Hold the pencil between your palms.
8. Move your hands back and forth to make the paper sphere spin.

RESULTS While the sphere is spinning, the top and bottom of the strips flatten slightly, and the center bulges.

WHY? The spinning sphere has a force that tends to move the paper strips outward, causing the top and bottom to flatten. Earth, like all rotating spheres, bulges at the center and has some flattening at the poles. The difference between the distance around Earth at the equator and the distance around Earth at the poles is about 42 miles (67.2 km).

TILT

PURPOSE: To demonstrate the effect of Earth's tilt on seasons.

MATERIALS:
- ball of modeling clay the size of an apple
- 2 pencils
- flashlight

PROCEDURE:

1. Insert a pencil through the ball of clay.

2. Use the second pencil to mark the equator line around the center of the clay ball. This line should be halfway between the top and bottom of the ball.

11

3. Position the ball on a table so that the pencil eraser is leaning slightly to the right.

4. In a darkened room, place the flashlight about 6 in. (15 cm) from the left side of the ball.

5. Observe where the light strikes the ball.

6. Place the light about 6 in. (15 cm) from the right side of the clay ball.

7. Observe where the light strikes the ball.

RESULTS The area below the equator receives the most light when the pencil eraser points away from the light, and the area above the equator is brighter when the pencil eraser points toward the light.

WHY? The pencil represents the imaginary axis running through Earth. The Northern Hemisphere, the area above the equator, is warmed the most when Earth's axis points toward the sun. This is because more direct light rays hit the area. The Southern Hemisphere, the area below the equator, receives the warming direct light rays when Earth's axis points away from the sun. The direction of Earth's axis changes very slightly during Earth's movement around the sun, causing the Southern and Northern Hemispheres to receive different amounts of light rays. This results in a change of seasons.

MEGA-WEIGHT

PURPOSE: To demonstrate the difference in the weight of the atmosphere, hydrosphere, and lithosphere.

MATERIALS:

- 1 large paper clip
- cardboard, 4 inches × 12 inches (10 cm × 30 cm)
- 2 rubber bands
- pencil
- paper cup, 7 oz. (210 ml)
- 12-inch (30 cm) string
- marker
- soil

PROCEDURE:

1. Attach the paper clip to the top of the cardboard piece.

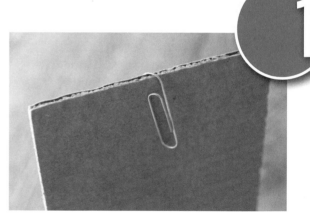

2. Tie the rubber bands together and hang them on the paper clip.

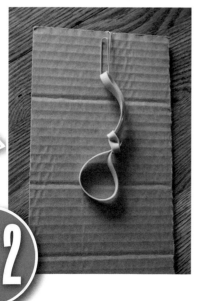

3. Use a pencil to punch two holes under the rim of the cup on opposite sides.
4. Run the string through the loop of the rubber band and tie the ends through each hole in the cup.
5. Hold the cardboard vertically so that the cup hangs freely.

6. Let the bottom of the lower rubber band be the pointer. Mark the position of the pointer and label the mark "Air."
7. Fill the cup with water.
8. Mark the position of the pointer and label the mark "Water."

9. Empty the cup and refill it with soil.

10. Mark the position of the pointer and label the mark "Land."

RESULTS Comparing the weight of equal quantities of air, water, and soil indicates that air is the lightest and soil the heaviest material.

WHY? The soil used in the experiment does not contain all of the elements found in the lithosphere. The lithosphere is the outer part of Earth not including the air above Earth (the atmosphere) or the water on Earth (the hydrosphere). This experiment indicates that soil is heavier than air or water. If all three areas could be weighed, the lithosphere would make up most of the total weight, and the atmosphere would make up the least.

DEPOSITS

PURPOSE: To demonstrate the formation of caliche deposits.

MATERIALS:

- pickling lime (found with food canning supplies)
- 1 large-mouthed jar, 1 qt. (1 liter)
- measuring spoon, teaspoon (5 ml)
- masking tape
- marking pen

PROCEDURE:

1. Fill the jar half full with water.

2. Add ½ teaspoon (2.5 ml) of lime to the water and stir.

17

3

3. Place a piece of tape down the side of the jar.

4. Mark the height of the liquid in the jar with the marking pen.

4

5. Set the jar so that it will remain undisturbed.

6. Observe the jar daily for two weeks.

RESULTS The water level drops, and a white crusty deposit forms above the water line on the inside of the jar.

WHY? Like the jar of limewater, ground water contains large amounts of minerals, including calcium. When carbon dioxide gas from the air dissolves in the mineral water, a white solid called calcium carbonate is formed. As the water evaporates, a crust of white calcium carbonate is left. Large deposits of calcium carbonate are found in the semiarid southwestern United States. These deposits, known as caliche, are found on or near the surface of the ground.

DRIPPER

PURPOSE: To demonstrate the formation of stalagmites and stalactites.

MATERIALS:

- Epsom salts
- 2 small jars, such as baby food jars
- cotton string
- scissors
- 2 washers
- spoon
- ruler
- paper

PROCEDURE:

1. Fill each jar with Epsom salts.

1

2. Add water to the height of the Epsom salts.

3. Stir.
4. Cut a piece of string, 24 in. (60 cm).
5. Tie a washer to each end of the string.

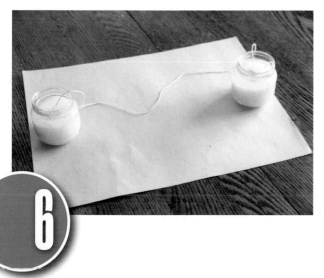

6. Place one washer in each of the jars.

7. Place a piece of paper between the jars.

8. Position the jars so that the string hangs between them with the lowest part of the loop about 1 in. (2.5 cm) above the paper.

9. Allow the jars to stand undisturbed and out of any draft for one week. Observe the changes to the washers.

RESULTS Part of the Epsom salt does not dissolve in the water, and the washers rest on top of the undissolved crystals. Water drips from the center of the loop onto the paper. A hard, white crust forms on the string and grows downward as time passes. A mound of white crystals builds up on the paper beneath the string.

WHY? Water containing the Epsom salts moves through the string. As the water evaporates, crystals of Epsom salts are deposited. The Epsom salt formations are just models of how crystal deposits form in caves. Actually, calcium found in ground water mixes with carbonic acid (rainwater plus carbon dioxide from the air), which seeps through the roof of the caves. As the water falls, small particles of calcium carbonate cling to the ceiling, eventually forming long spikes called stalactites. The water that reaches the floor evaporates, leaving the calcium carbonate deposits, which build to form stalagmites. The formation of these rocklike icicles is a very slow process; it takes many thousands of years for them to form.

WASH AWAY

PURPOSE: To demonstrate hydraulic mining.

MATERIALS:

- empty coffee can
- 10 paper clips
- small pebbles—enough to line the bottom of the can
- 1 cup (250 ml) of soil
- garden hose with spray nozzle

PROCEDURE:

Note: This is an outdoor activity.

1. Place the paper clips, pebbles, and soil in the can.

2. Mix thoroughly.

23

3

3. Place the can outside on the ground.

5

4. Set the water nozzle on the high pressure position.

5. Direct the stream of water into the can.

6. Continue to spray the water into the can until the overflow water looks clean.

6

RESULTS The dirt is washed out of the can, leaving the pebbles and paper clips in the bottom of the can.

WHY? Some of the soil dissolves in the water, and some of it is light enough to be lifted and carried out of the can by the moving water. The paper clips and pebbles are too hard to be broken apart by the spraying water like the dirt particles. The heavier materials are not lifted by the water, so they remain in the bottom of the can. Rocks that contain metal are called ores. Ore deposits are mined with water. Powerful streams of water are used to wash away the soil surrounding the ore. The rock pieces left are taken to refining plants where pure metals are removed. The process of mining with water is called hydraulic mining.

PRINTS

PURPOSE: To determine how fossils were preserved.

MATERIALS:

- paper plate
- paper cup
- modeling clay
- seashell

- petroleum jelly
- plaster of Paris
- plastic spoon

PROCEDURE:

1. Place a piece of clay about the size of a lemon on the paper plate.

2. Rub the outside of the seashell with petroleum jelly.

3. Press the seashell into the clay.

4. Carefully remove the seashell so that a clear imprint of the shell remains in the clay.

5. Mix four spoons of plaster of Paris with two spoons of water in the paper cup.

6. Pour the plaster mixture into the imprint in the clay. Throw the paper cup and spoon away.

7. Allow the plaster to harden, about fifteen to twenty minutes.

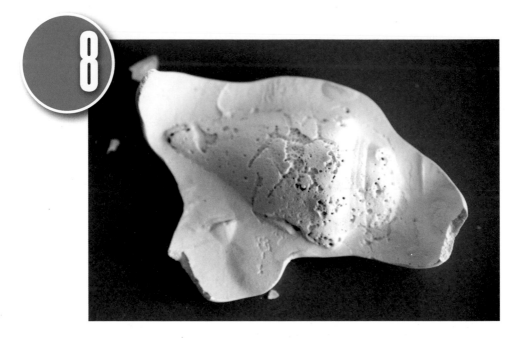

8. Separate the clay from the plaster mold.

RESULTS The clay has an imprint of the outside of the shell, and the plaster looks like the outside of the shell.

WHY? The layer of clay and the plaster are both examples of fossils. The clay represents the soft mud of ancient times. Organisms made imprints in the mud. If nothing collected in the prints, the mud dried, forming what is now called a cast fossil. When sediments filled the imprint, a sedimentary rock formed with the print of the organism on the outside. This type of fossil is called a mold fossil.

RUB-A-DUB

PURPOSE: To demonstrate the effect of heat produced by crustal movement.

MATERIALS:

- cardboard
- glass soft-drink bottle
- scissors
- refrigerator
- cup of water

PROCEDURE:

1. Cut a circle from the cardboard that is slightly larger than the top of the bottle.

2. Place the empty bottle in the freezer for twenty minutes.

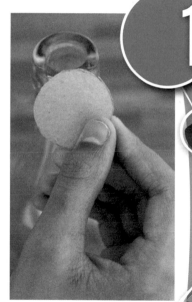

3. Remove the bottle from the freezer.

29

4. Dip the cardboard into the cup of water and place the wet paper over the mouth of the bottle.

5. Quickly rub the palms of your hands together twenty times.

6. Immediately place your hands around the outside of the bottle.

RESULTS One side of the cardboard circle rises and falls.

WHY? The moving and colliding of molecules emits heat energy. Rubbing your hands together produces heat, and this heat causes the cold air in the bottle to warm up and expand. This expanded gas pushes up on the paper with enough force to partially lift the paper and allow the hot gas to escape.

When sections of Earth's crust rub against each other as they move, the heat produced causes the rock material to vibrate. If molecules in the solid rock move fast enough, they break away from each other, and the solid melts into magma (liquid rock beneath the ground). Further heating can cause the liquid to change into a gas. Most materials become larger when heated. Crustal changes such as earthquakes and volcanoes occur when materials inside Earth expand, forcing heat, energy, and gaseous materials out through its surface.

POP TOP

PURPOSE: To demonstrate how a geyser works.

MATERIALS:

- funnel
- large coffee can or pot as tall as the funnel
- plastic tubing about 1 yd. (1 m) long

PROCEDURE:

1. Set the funnel mouth down into the pot.

2. Fill the pot with water.

3. Place the end of the plastic tubing under the rim of the funnel.

4

4. Blow into the tubing.

RESULTS Water sprays out of the funnel's tube.

WHY? Blowing air under the funnel forces air bubbles up the stem of the funnel. As the air moves upward, it pushes water out the top of the tube. Geysers are funnel-shaped cracks in the ground that are filled by underground streams. When water in the lower part of the crack is heated to boiling, the bubbles of steam rise to the surface. A geyser erupts when water trapped in the neck of the funnel-shaped crack is forced out the top by the rising bubbles of steam. As long as you continue to blow under the funnel, water erupts out the top, but natural geysers erupt only when enough pressure builds up to force the water up and out the top of the crack. Some geysers erupt once every few minutes, while others erupt only once every few years. Old Faithful in Yellowstone National Park is an example of a geyser that erupts so regularly that a schedule of its display can be listed. This geyser erupts about every seventy minutes and has not missed an eruption in more than eighty years of observations. Geysers are rare; most of the world's geysers are in Iceland, New Zealand, and Yellowstone National Park.

SPREADER

PURPOSE: To demonstrate the expansion of the Mid-Atlantic Ridge.

MATERIALS:

- scissors
- shoe box
- modeling clay
- sheet of paper

PROCEDURE:

1. Cut two 3 in. × 11 in. (7 cm × 28 cm) strips from a sheet of paper.

2. Cut out a 0.5 in. × 3.5 in. (1 cm × 9 cm) section from the center of the bottom of the shoe box.

3. Cut out a section in the center of one of the box's largest sides.

4. Put the paper strips together, and run them up through the slit in the box.

5. Pull the strips out about 3.5 in. (9 cm), and fold them back on opposite sides.

6. Press a flattened strip of modeling clay about the size of a pencil on the end of each strip.

7. Hold the papers under the box between your index finger and second finger.

8. Slowly push the strips up though the slit.

Results The clay pieces move away from each other as more paper moves upward.

WHY? The clay represents old seafloor bordering the Mid-Atlantic Ridge. The rising paper acts like the hot, molten rock moving out of the crack in the mid-ocean ridge. When liquid rock pushes through the ocean floor's surface, it forms a new layer on both sides of the crack. It is believed that this new material pushes against the old floor, causing it to spread. The Mid-Atlantic Ridge may be widening by about 1 in. (2.5 cm) each year.

SWINGERS

PURPOSE: To determine if the north end of a magnet always points to Earth's magnetic North Pole.

MATERIALS:

- compass
- sewing thread
- 2 steel straight pins
- cellophane tape

- scissors
- paper
- ruler
- magnet

PROCEDURE:

1. Place the heads of the pins on the ends of the magnet so that their points face each other.

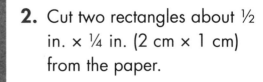

2. Cut two rectangles about ½ in. × ¼ in. (2 cm × 1 cm) from the paper.

3. Cut a 12 in. (30 cm) and a 24 in. (60 cm) piece of thread.

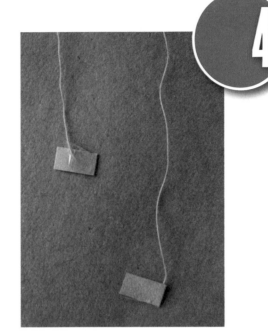

4. Attach one thread to each of the rectangular pieces of paper.

5. Insert one pin in each of the pieces of paper.

6. Tape the ends of the threads to the top of a door opening, about 12 in. (30 cm) apart.

7. Observe the direction in which the heads of the pins point.

8. Use a compass to determine the direction the pins are pointing.

RESULTS The head of one pin points south and the other points north.

WHY? Earth behaves as if a large bar magnet is inside it causing magnetic materials to be attracted to its opposite ends. The north end of this imaginary magnet produces Earth's north magnetic pole, and the north ends of all magnets are attracted to this pole. The north ends of magnets are really north-seeking poles. You are temporarily lining up the electrons in the pins when you put them in contact with a magnet. Placing the pins on the magnet in opposite directions causes the head of one pin and the point of the other pin to be north-seeking poles.

DETECTOR

PURPOSE: To demonstrate how a seismogram is produced.

MATERIALS:

- jar with a lid, 1 qt. (1 liter)
- wide-point, felt-tip pen
- rubber band
- masking tape
- scissors
- wax paper
- ruler

PROCEDURE:

1. Fill the jar with water and close the lid.
2. Cut a 6 in. × 12 in. (15 cm × 30 cm) strip of wax paper.

3. Lay the wax paper on a table.

4. Set the jar of water on one end of the wax paper.
5. Attach the pen to the jar, point down, with a rubber band.

6. Position the pen so that the felt tip touches the wax paper, then tape the pen to the jar.

7. Hold the free end of the paper, and push the paper close to the jar.

8. Quickly and with force pull the paper straight out from under the jar.

RESULTS The pen marks a line on the paper as the paper moves from under the stationary jar.

WHY? Inertia is the resistance to a change in motion. Inertia increases with mass. The mass of the water-filled jar is great, and thus the inertia of the jar holds it steady while the paper moves out from under it. A seismograph has a suspended mass that holds steady, while the stand to which it is attached moves when vibrated. A pen is attached to the stationary mass with its point lightly touching the stand. Vibrations move the stand but not the pen, so the pen draws a line back and forth on the vibrating stand. A wavy line would be recorded if during an earthquake a sheet of paper were pulled slowly between the pen and the vibrating stand. This written record is called a seismogram. The line drawn by your homemade seismograph is straight because the table on which the jar sat was not vibrating. Straight-line seismograms indicate the absence of earthquakes.

RUN OFF

PURPOSE: To demonstrate how rain affects topsoil.

MATERIALS:

- dirt
- red powdered tempera paint
- measuring spoon, teaspoon (5 ml)
- funnel
- coffee filter paper
- wide-mouthed jar, 1 qt. (1 liter)
- measuring cup, 1 cup (250 ml)
- stirring spoon

PROCEDURE:

1. Add ¼ teaspoon (1.25 ml) of red tempera paint to ¼ cup (75 ml) of dirt. Mix thoroughly.

2. Set the funnel in the jar.

3. Place the coffee filter inside the funnel.

4. Pour the colored sand into the paper filter.

5. Add ¼ cup (75 ml) of water to the funnel.

6. Observe the water dripping into the jar.

7. Pour this water out of the jar and add another ¼ cup (75 ml) of water to the funnel.

RESULTS The liquid dripping out of the funnel is red.

WHY? The red paint represents nutrients in topsoil that are soluble in water. Nutrients dissolve in rainwater and feed the plants growing in the soil. If the rain is too heavy, the water runs across the land, taking the dissolved nutrients with it. Excessive rains can leave the topsoil lacking in necessary nutrients.

SPEEDY

PURPOSE: To demonstrate how the speed of running water affects erosion.

MATERIALS:

- pencil
- paper cup
- drinking straw
- modeling clay
- cardboard about 1 ft (30 cm) square
- dirt
- 1 gallon (4 liter) jar filled with water

PROCEDURE:

Note: This is an outdoor activity.

1. Use the pencil to make a hole in the side of the paper cup near the bottom rim.

2. Cut the straw in half and insert one of the pieces in the hole in the cup.

3. Use the clay to form a seal around the hole.

4. Lay the cardboard on the ground and raise one end about 2 in. (5 cm) by putting dirt under the edge of the cardboard.

5. Cover the cardboard with a thin layer of dirt.

6. Set the cup on the raised end of the dirt with the straw pointing downhill.

7. Hold your finger over the end of the straw as you fill the cup with water.
8. Open the straw and observe the movement of the water.
9. Clean the cardboard and cover it again with dirt.
10. Raise the end of the cardboard about 6 in. (15 cm).
11. Place the cup at the top of the incline.
12. Cover the straw with your finger as you fill the cup with water.

13. Release the straw and observe the water movement.

13

RESULTS Dirt is washed down the incline by the running water. More dirt is washed away when the slope of the cardboard is increased.

WHY? As the slope increases, the water flows more quickly. The energy of the flowing water increases with speed. Moving water hits against the dirt and pushes it forward. The faster the water moves, the more energy it has, and thus the more dirt it pushes forward.

EXPERIMENT 15 FLY AWAY

PURPOSE: To determine how moisture affects land erosion.

MATERIALS:

- paper hole punch
- sheet of paper
- shallow baking pan
- bowl of water

PROCEDURE:

1. Cut fifty paper circles from the paper with the paper hole punch.

2. Place the paper circles in the pan at one end.

50

3. Blow across the paper circles.

4. Wet your fingers in the bowl of water and sprinkle the water over the paper circles. You want the paper to be damp.

5

5. Blow across the paper circles again.

RESULTS The dry paper particles easily move to the opposite end of the pan and some fly out of the pan. The wet paper does not move easily.

WHY? Loose, lightweight particles can be picked up by the wind and carried for long distances. Flyaway surface particles that are easily supported by the wind are commonly found in deserts and along shorelines. The damp paper circles stick together and are too heavy for your breath to lift. Damp land areas and those covered by vegetation are not as easily eroded by the wind because, like the damp paper, the materials are too heavy to be lifted by the wind.

UP AND DOWN

PURPOSE: To determine how erosion causes mountains to rise.

MATERIALS:

- wooden block 2 in. × 4 in. × 2 in. (5 cm × 10 cm × 5 cm)
- see-through container about twice as large as the wooden block
- sand
- masking tape
- marking pen
- ruler
- tablespoon (15 ml)

PROCEDURE:

1. Fill the container about one-half full with water.

2. Place a piece of tape down the side of the container.

3. Start at the top of the tape and mark it off in centimeters.

4. Place a piece of tape down the side of the wooden block and mark it off in centimeters.

5. Place the wooden block in the container of water.

6. Pour one spoon of sand on top of the block.

7. Observe the water level on the block and in the container.

8. Use the spoon to scrape the sand from the top of the block into the water.

9

9. Observe the water level on the block and in the container.

RESULTS The wooden block floats higher in the water when the sand is removed, but the water level in the container stays the same.

WHY? The water level is forced upward by the weight of the sand and the wooden block. Removing the sand from the block decreases the weight of the block, allowing it to float higher in the water. Moving the sand from the block to the water does not change the total weight in the bowl, so the water level in the container remains the same. This same balance is achieved by the erosion of mountains. The weight of the mountain decreases and it floats higher on the mantle as materials are washed into the ocean. The weight of the added sediment along the seacoast causes the crust below it to sink. The mountain rises and the ocean crust sinks. This equal up-and-down movement of Earth's crust is called isostasy.

COLD 'N HOT

PURPOSE: To determine how Earth's heat level remains constant.

MATERIALS:

- 2 thermometers
- 2 plastic bags, 1 large and 1 small, with twist ties

PROCEDURE:

1. Lay one thermometer inside the small bag.

1

2

2. Inflate the bag by blowing into it, then close the end with the twist tie.
3. Put the inflated bag inside the larger plastic bag.
4. Inflate the large bag with air and close the end with the twist tie.

5. Place the bag in direct sunlight, and lay the second thermometer next to the bag.

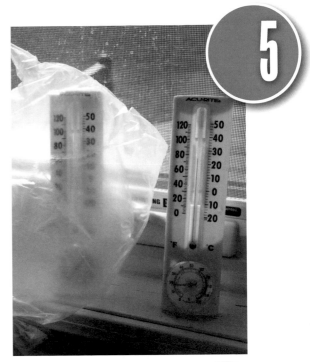

6. Observe the temperature reading of both thermometers after thirty minutes.

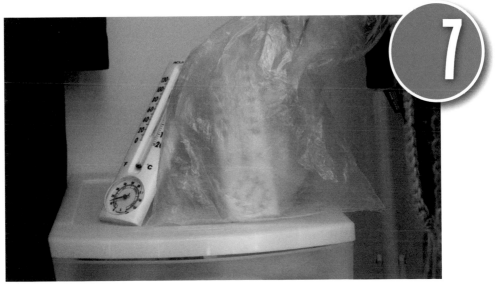

7. Move the bag and free thermometer to a dark closet.

8. Observe the temperature reading on both thermometers after thirty minutes.

RESULTS In the sunlight, the thermometer reading inside the bag was higher, and it changed more slowly after being placed in the dark area.

WHY? The double layer of air inside the bag acts like a greenhouse, as does the atmosphere around Earth. Both envelopes of air allow radiant energy from the sun to enter, and the resulting heat energy is trapped. Sunlight enters Earth's atmosphere, and this radiation is absorbed by plants and soil, which change it into heat energy. Heat energy is radiated from Earth's surface toward space, but the gases in the atmosphere absorb and reradiate the heat back toward Earth. The air inside the plastic bags similarly reradiates the heat, thus keeping the temperature inside warmer. Earth's atmosphere, like the air bags, acts as an insulator, holding on to the heat absorbed from the sun during the daytime. This trapped energy inside the atmosphere is constantly being moved from one place to the other, which prevents extreme differences in day and night temperatures. Without this protective layer of air, Earth would get very hot during the day and very cold at night.

BREEZES

PURPOSE: To determine the cause of land and sea breezes.

MATERIALS:

- ruler
- 2 thermometers
- 2 glasses large enough to hold the thermometers
- desk lamp
- dirt

PROCEDURE:

1. Pour 2 in. (6 cm) of water into a glass.

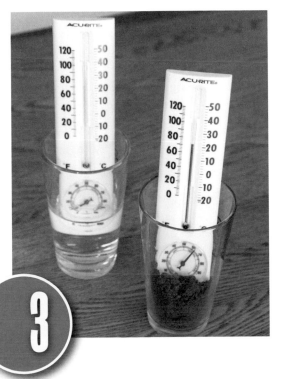

2. Pour 2 in. (5 cm) of dirt into the second glass.
3. Place a thermometer in each glass.

59

5

4. Set the glasses together on a table and allow them to stand for thirty minutes before recording the reading on each thermometer.

5. Position the lamp so that the light evenly hits both glasses.

6. Record the temperature on each thermometer after one hour.

6

7. Turn the light off.

8. Record the temperature on each thermometer after one hour.

RESULTS The temperature of the dirt increases more than the water, and the dirt cools faster than does the water.

WHY? The difference in the time it takes land and water to change temperature affects the movement of air above it. During the day, the land heats more quickly than the ocean. Hot air above the land rises, and cooler air above the water rushes in to take the place of the rising warm air. This air movement is called a sea breeze. At night the land cools faster than the water. The hotter air above the water rises, and the cooler air above the land rushes toward the ocean. This is called a land breeze.

19 MORE OR LESS

PURPOSE: To determine the effects of surface temperature on dew formation.

MATERIALS:

- clock
- glass bottle
- jar large enough for the bottle to fit inside
- ice
- paper towels

PROCEDURE:

1. Wrap your hands around the bottle and hold it for two minutes. You want as much of your skin to touch the glass as possible.

1

2. Exhale on the outside of the bottle.

3. Observe the surface of the bottle.

4. Fill the jar one-half full with water and add four to five ice cubes.

5. Set the bottle in the icy water for two minutes.

6. Remove the bottle and dry the outside with a paper towel.

7. Exhale on the outside of the bottle.

RESULTS The surface of the warm bottle clouds over when the exhaled breath touches it, but the cloud quickly disappears, leaving a dry surface. The cloud formed on the cold bottle by the exhaled breath turns into tiny drops of water. The entire surface of the cold bottle clouds if the humidity of the air is high.

WHY? Water vapor from your exhaled breath condenses (changes into a liquid) on the surface of both bottles. The warm surface supplies energy for the tiny water droplets to quickly evaporate (change into a vapor). The tiny droplets on the cold surface group together, forming large drops of water. Cold surfaces collect more water drops (dew) than do warmer surfaces. If the surface is too warm, water vapor in the air striking the surface will not condense at all, and if there is a collection of moisture, it quickly evaporates.

VANISHING WATER

PURPOSE: To determine why lakes dry up.

MATERIALS:

- 2 glass jars, one with a lid
- masking tape
- marking pen

PROCEDURE:

1. Put a strip of tape down the side of both jars from top to bottom.

2. Fill both jars half full with water.

65

3

3. Use the marking pen to mark the top of the water level on each strip of tape.

4. Seal one jar with a lid and leave the second jar open.

4

5. Allow the jars to sit undisturbed for two weeks.

6. Observe the level of the water in each jar and mark the new level if there is a change.

RESULTS The level of the water in the open jar is lower, and the water level in the closed jar is unchanged. On some days, the closed jar looked cloudy, and drops of water cling to the inside of the glass.

WHY? Liquid water molecules on the surface of water absorb enough energy from the surrounding air to change into a vapor. In the open jar, like any body of water exposed to the open air, water molecules on the surface vaporize and move upward into the atmosphere. As each water molecule vaporizes and leaves, the level of the water decreases. Surface water vaporized in the closed jar, but it was not able to escape. The vapor condensed (changed back into a liquid) as it hit the cool surface of the jar. The rising vapor above a lake or any body of water condenses when cooled, but the water droplets can be carried to other areas by moving wind. Lakes dry up when the evaporating surface water does not return in the form of rain.

TORNADO

PURPOSE: To demonstrate the appearance of a tornado.

MATERIALS:

- 2 plastic, 2-qt. (2-liter) soft-drink bottles
- duct tape
- scissors
- pencil
- paper towels
- ruler

PROCEDURE:

1. Fill one bottle half full with water.

2. Cut a strip of tape about 1 in. × 2 in. (2.5 cm × 5 cm).

3. Cover the mouth of the bottle containing water with the strip of tape.

4. Use the pencil to punch a hole in the center of the tape. Make the hole slightly larger than the pencil.

5. Use your fingers to smooth and secure the edges of the tape around the hole in the tape.

6. Turn the second bottle so that the mouth of each bottle lines up.

7. Use a paper towel to dry any moisture from the necks of the bottles.

8. Wrap strips of tape around the necks of the bottles to secure them tightly.

9. Flip the bottles so that the bottle with the water is on top. Grasp the bottles around the necks and quickly swirl them in circles parallel to the floor.

10. Set the bottles on a table, with the empty one on the bottom.

RESULTS The water swirls in a funnel shape as it pours from the top bottle. The falling water looks like a tornado.

WHY? The funnel-shaped water moves through the small hole similar to the spiraling tail of a wind tornado. The water movement is due to the action of several forces, as is the movement of a tornado. Tornadoes in the United States form along fronts between cool, dry air from the West and warm, humid air from the Gulf of Mexico. The warm air quickly rushes upward, causing winds to rotate violently. Drops of water are formed as the water vapor condenses due to the low temperature and pressure inside the funnel. Tornadoes are visible because the large amount of liquid water in the cloud blocks the light as it does in a thundercloud. The debris picked up from the ground by the swirling winds adds to the color of the funnel cloud.

CURRENTS

PURPOSE: To determine if temperature affects the motion of water.

MATERIALS:
- blue food coloring
- 2 clear drinking glasses
- 2 coffee cups
- jar, 1 quart (liter)
- eyedropper
- ice

1

PROCEDURE:

1. Fill the jar half full with ice, then add water to fill the jar. Allow to stand for five minutes.

2. Fill one of the cups one-quarter full with the cold water from the jar.

3

3. Add enough food coloring to the cold water to produce a dark blue liquid.

4. Fill one of the glasses with hot water from the faucet.

5. Fill the eyedropper with the cold colored water.

6

6. Insert the tip of the eyedropper into the hot water in the glass and release several drops of colored water.

7. Observe the movement of the colored water.

8. Fill the second glass with cold water from the jar.

9. Fill the remaining cup one-quarter full with hot water from the faucet and add enough food coloring to produce a dark blue liquid.

10. Fill the eyedropper with the hot colored water.

11. Insert the tip of the eyedropper in the cold water in the glass. Release several drops of the hot colored water.

12. Observe the movement of the colored water.

RESULTS The hot colored water rose in the cold water, and the cold colored water sank in the hot water.

WHY? Cold water contracts (gets closer together). Hot water expands (moves farther apart). This makes a drop of cold water more dense than a drop of hot water because the molecules occupy less space. The denser cold water sinks and the less dense hot water rises. Convection currents are the results of water and air movement due to changes in temperature.

GLOSSARY

atmosphere The layer of air above Earth.

caliche (ka leé chee) Deposits of limestone (calcium carbonate) near or on the surface of the ground.

cloud Mass of tiny raindrops in the sky.

contract To move closer together.

current A flow of moving water or air.

dew Moisture condensed from the air.

erosion Wearing away.

expand To move farther apart.

fossil Any impression or trace of organisms from past
geologic times.

geyser A funnel-shaped crack in the ground that periodically
throws out jets of hot water and steam.

hydraulic mining Using powerful streams of water to mine
metal.

hydrosphere Water on the surface of Earth.

isostasy The equal up-and-down movement of Earth's crust.

lithosphere The solid part of Earth.

magma The liquid rock beneath Earth's surface.

mantle The middle layer of Earth located beneath the upper
crust.

mid-ocean ridge Mountain chain on the floor of the ocean
from which magma rises and causes seafloor spreading.

ore A rock with enough metal content to make it profitable to
extract.

rotate To spin on one's own axis, as a wheel turns on
an axis.

sedimentary rock A rock made of layers of sediments that have been cemented together.

seismogram The written record from a seismograph.

thermometer An instrument used to measure temperature.

topsoil The upper soil surface that is rich in nutrients and minerals.

volcano A mountain from which steam, ash, and lava are expelled through openings.

wind The movement of air.

Alaska Volcano Observatory
903 Koyukuk Drive
Fairbanks, AK 99775-6020
(907) 474-1542
Web site: http://www.wovo.org
This is the American branch of the World Organization of
    Volcano Observatories. It is in charge of volcano surveil-
    lance and warning authorities and the public about
    volcanic unrest.

American Association for the Advancement of Science
1200 New York Avenue NW
Washington, DC 20005
(202) 326-6400
Web site: http://www.aaas.org
This international nonprofit organization is dedicated to
    advancing science around the world by serving as an
    educator, leader, spokesperson, and professional
    association.

American Museum of Natural History
Central Park West at 79th Street
New York, NY 10024-5192
(212) 769-5100
Web site: http://www.amnh.org
This museum showcases hundreds of animal species and
    fossils from the history of life on Earth.

Colorado School of Mines Geology Museum
General Research Laboratory Building
1310 Maple Street
Golden, CO 80401
(303) 273-3815
Web site: http://www.mines.edu/Geology_Museum
E-mail: geomuseum@mines.edu
This museum displays mineral, fossil, gemstone, meteorite, and historic mining artifacts.

Geological Society of America
P.O. Box 9140
Boulder, CO 80301-9140
(303) 357-1070
Web site: http://www.geosociety.org
This organization provides access to elements that are essential to the professional growth of earth scientists at all levels of expertise and from all sectors: academic, government, business, and industry.

Web Sites

Due to the changing nature of Internet links, Rosen Publishing has developed an online list of Web sites related to the subject of this book. This site is updated regularly. Please use this link to access the list:

http://www.rosenlinks.com/Scif/esci

FOR FURTHER READING

Allaby, Michael. *National Geographic Visual Encyclopedia of Earth*. Des Moines, IA: National Geographic Children's Books, 2008.

Brown, Cynthia Light. *Geology of the Pacific Northwest: Investigate How the Earth Was Formed*. White River Junction, VT: Nomad Press, 2011.

Chancellor, Deborah. *Science Kids: Planet Earth*. New York, NY: Kingfisher, 2008.

Claybourne, Anna, Gillian Doherty, and Rebecca Treays. *The Usborne Encyclopedia of Planet Earth*. London, UK: Usborne, 2009.

Cosgrove, Brian. *Weather*. New York, NY: DK, 2007.

Denecke, Edward J., Jr. *Painless Earth Science*. New York, NY: Barron's, 2011.

DK Publishing. *First Earth Encyclopedia*. New York: DK, 2010.

Faulkner, Rebecca. *Crystals*. Mankato, MN: Heinemann-Raintree, 2008.

Gray, Susan Heinrichs. *Geology: The Study of Rocks*. Danbury, CT: Children's Press, 2012.

Landau, Elaine. *Earth*. Danbury, CT: Children's Press, 2008.

Oxlade, Chris. *Hands-on Science Projects: Earth*. Lanham, MD: Anness, 2009.

Snedden, Robert. *Earth's Shifting Surface*. Mankato, MN: Heinemann-Raintree, 2009.

TIME for Kids. *Big Book of Science Experiments: A Step-by-Step Guide*. New York, NY: Time for Kids, 2011.

Van Rose, Susanna. *Earth*. New York, NY: DK, 2005.

INDEX

About the Author

Janice VanCleave is a former school science teacher and a captivating presenter at museums, schools, and bookstores nationwide. She is the author of more than twenty other science books for children.

Designer: Nicole Russo; Editor: Bethany Bryan

All photos by Renée C. Veniskey. Cover and p. 1 background © istockphoto.com/Mustafa Deliormanli.